I'M ACCEPTED

WALKing the Journey

from Rejection to Freedom

Blessing on the journey!

Holland Nance

Holland B. Nance

Bible versions used in this book are as follows:

Publisher information

Copyright © 2016 by Holland B. Nance, LLC

All rights reserved. Published 2016

Printed in the United States of America

Edited by Adam Colwell
Cover design by Virtual Illustrations

Printing and distribution by IngramSpark

ISBN: 978-0-9969203-9-1

www.hollandnance.com

CONTENTS

Section 1—Before the WALK Began • 11

Section 2—Let's Take the WALK Together • 43

Section 3—WALK or BEND • 97

Section 4—WALKing in Wisdom • 121

Section 5—An Open Letter to Fathers • 141

ACKNOWLEDGMENTS

I am thankful to the Most High God for allowing me the privilege of completing this assignment and sharing my testimony regarding one of the most impactful parts of my life. I give all praise and glory to Him.

Thank you to all of the friends who have endured listening to me talk about this writing project throughout the years. I really appreciate you all remaining supportive and prayerful through this process.

I am very grateful for my aunt (who took me in and cared for me after my mother passed away), Barbara R. Mitchell and all of my family who continue to encourage me to do all that God has given me to do.

Thank you to Rev. Dr. Michael L. and Rev. Twanna Henderson (New Beginnings Church, Matthews, NC) for training me and allowing me to exhibit my true love for ministry and serving others. Also to Pastors Demetrius and Angela Miles (Tucson

Church International), thank you for your love, support, and making me a part of the TCI family in such a short time.

Thank you to my editor and writing coach, Adam Colwell, who help me accomplish more than I ever thought was possible.

To the memory of my mother, the late Lillie R. Nance, my father, the late John H. Nance, my uncle (who took me in after mom passed away), the late William H. Mitchell, Sr., my brother, the late James L. Nance, Sr. Each of their legacies will remain on this Earth because they took the time to love and care for so many people, especially me.

FOREWORD

Disappointment, heartbreaks, and rejections are all too familiar life experiences. We have all been disappointed, heartbroken, or rejected at some point along our life's journey. So, the question is not have you experienced disappointment, heartbreak, or rejection, it is how have you navigated through these life experiences? Have you attempted to mask or completely ignore the catastrophic impact of these experiences? Have you allowed these negative experiences to debilitate or liberate you?

The timing of this book is impeccable because of the increasingly subtle or severe rejection occurring all around us through traditional means of family, friends, work environments and now we have social media added to the mix that has allowed rejection to take on a new identity and intensity. Today, rejection is not always private experience; it can be a "like", "don't like", or a written message that is seen by the world.

Holland B. Nance has done a masterful job of shedding light on the pain and the process of healing of such a deadly negative emotion. In the pages of this book, you will find a front row seat to Holland's personal journey from disappointment, heartbreak, and rejection, to healing and wholeness. I applaud Holland for sharing so transparently her wounds and process of healing. You will find scholarly and practical insights to apply wherever you find yourself on the journey.

It has been my great honor to serve in public ministry for thirty years and I have been privileged to engage with a countless number of people. As I counseled with people through their deepest pain and challenges, I have discovered that for many the root cause was rejection. I believe rejection to be so toxic because rejection never stops at rejection. When people experience rejection, it has the tendency to lead the person being rejected to reject themselves, it is not the perpetrator of rejection but the recipient of rejection who causes the greatest negative impact. I am in no way excusing the perpetrator but desire to expose the end goal of rejection, which is self-destruction by causing people to diminish their self-esteem. At the core of self-esteem is a person's identity. This book provides a clear process for you to discover, establish, and thrive in your true identity—and Holland intentionally and gently encourages you to find your true identity in Jesus Christ. "I have been crucified with Christ and I no longer live, but Christ lives in me. The life I now live in the body, I live by faith in the Son of God, who loved me and gave himself for me." (Galatians 2:20 NIV)

Rejection is toxic and a deadly negative emotion, but it does not have to triumph in your life. I want to encourage you to take this journey with Holland so you can have a personal testimony of climbing out of the clinches of rejection and learning how to live a life of freedom and healing. The best is still yet to come for your life!

Demetrius Miles
Senior Pastor
Tucson Church International

DEDICATION

I wrote this book for your who have been impacted by the pain of disappointment, heartbreak, and rejection; to the ones who have been mistreated by those who should have cared the most, and to those whose value has been questions and under-appreciated.

This book is for you – you are not alone. Whether it was a rejection from other children during childhood, or rejection from an employer during adulthood, rejection can have debilitating effects on you emotionally, physically, and spiritually. Depending on the events of life, that rejection may have been brushed off easily, or it may have crippled the potential to move further beyond the initial point of pain.

One of the definitions of rejection is a "throwing back". Those who reject you, refuse to believe you, accept you, or consider you; they decide not be seen with you in public because you are not deemed good enough; they refuse to hear, receive, or admit you. All of these words and actions pale in comparison to the deep, long-standing results that will be experienced if the rejection is not managed and eradicated properly.

THE GOOD NEWS

Rejection is horrible and over times, the ways it displays itself in your life is horrific. I assure you, *there is hope*! These terrible effects of rejection can be overcome and you can move forward to experience the fullness and richness that life really has available for you.

In this book, I will share my personal experiences with rejection, heartbreak, and disappointment. More importantly, I will share a few points that may be helpful in your journey to freedom from rejection. I will guide you through the process to WALK the truth (Willfully Abandon Lies and Know the truth). This four-step process helped me during my own journey from rejection to freedom. This guide—along with prayer, faith, a strong determination to live at a higher level, and the power of God's grace—will assist you as you begin and progress through your own journey. There will be questions for you to consider as you read. I encourage you to journal your way through this process and review what you discover and uncover.

May this book envelop you. May its words embrace you with love, warmth, and empowerment. May each chapter wrap its arms around you and squeeze you until your heart is filled with wholeness and health. May it grab you by the shoulders, lift you up, and look you deep in the eyes of your soul to connect you to all of the power, beauty, and well-being that already exists within you.

May this book help you to know how valuable you are to God, and how much He loves you and wants you to believe in the *truth* of everything He knows and has said about you.

A journey is a continual process. Even now, I have to remind myself, consistently, to WALK the truth!

Now, let's WALK the truth together!

Holland B. Nance

Section 1

Before the WALK Began

Holland B. Nance

Part 1

MY STORY

One day he was there. The next day, he was gone.

Where did he go? Why did he leave? When will he be back? Will he be back?

He left me…without a single word or explanation. He didn't even offer to take me with him.

He just left me to go and live with that other lady. I know! It's because that other lady has a little boy.

Dad likes sons. He always spends time with my older brother, James and now he's gone to be with that other little boy. Dad doesn't like me—because I'm a girl. That's why he left me. Because I'm not a boy…I'm just a stupid girl.

That was the truth! Well, that's how it seemed back when my mother and father were divorced when I was five years old. All I knew was that my father was gone and my mother played the song, "Misty Blue" by Dorothy Moore on her eight-track player. The billowing sounds of the soulful melody, with my mother's soprano voice echoing the lyrics was the soundtrack of our home for many of those days. *Just the thought of you, tunes my whole world misty blue.* She played that song so much so that I still can sing the entire song word for word.

My father, a tall, handsome, and charismatic man who loved laughing, singing, preaching, and sharing the Gospel of Jesus Christ, was gone. Whether that was a choice he made on his own, or whether the choice was made for him, as a result of his behavior, I didn't know. All that mattered was, he was gone.

Life had to go on and sometimes, some conversations are just too difficult.

Mom and I were devastated. In the places where his booming voice and infectious laughter once filled the room, there was now quietness. At the end of the hallway, the place where I waited to hear his heavy footsteps as he entered our home, was now where I sat—hoping for his return. The chair at the table where he sat for meals was now abandoned, providing a clear view through the window into our backyard.

Dad was gone.

Mom and I did what was necessary to continue living, but a piece of our hearts had been snatched away. We both felt it, but there was no communication between us about it. We still sang and enjoyed music together. She still went to work where she taught elementary school. We still went to church on Sundays. But there was just no discussion about the change that impacted our lives in such a powerful way. Life had to go on and sometimes, some conversations are just too difficult.

Little did I know that at that time, the song was the only conversation my mother could express. Besides, who has time to sit down with a five-year-old to explain the idiosyncrasies of love, adultery, and divorce? Especially now that she was a single mother, working full-time, and having to manage the course of her life, while being unexpectedly alone. All I had left was to discuss it with myself.

"Why did he leave us?"

"What did I do to make him mad at us?"

"When will he come back? Maybe he'll be there today when I get back from school."

"Why won't he talk to me?"

"Why won't *anybody* tell me what's going on?"

Like most parents, my mother did not want to say terrible things to me about my father. Rather than saying that he was a despicable, lying philanderer, she chose to suppress the anger that she must have been feeling. She stayed silent on the subject, and gradually, with the sound of "Misty Blue" playing less often, life went on. For all of those questions that remained unanswered, my young mind had no problem filling in the blanks.

Those of us who have experienced divorce and/or loss of a parent tend to blame ourselves for the separation. Whether the child believes that they have done something "bad", or sees the separation as a personal rejection because of something about themselves that is beyond their control, there is still an abyss. It's filled with unanswered questions that the child answers with their own interpretation.

We take this self-blaming and convert it a feeling of rejection. The unexpected departure of a parent by death, divorce, or any other issues—leaves a child in emotional turmoil. In most cases, the child is provided with little to no information to help them fully understand the factors that are actually not at all related to them. All that is left is for us to make connections and develop reasoning based on the bits of information we are told and details that we capture upon observation. This creates feelings of abandonment and hinders levels of future relationships, trust, and self-worth. Without proper and complete communication, we ascribe explanations that inaccurately shape our worldview and self-image.

My abyss was filled with the belief that my father left to choose a woman with a son and, therefore, the only reason he left, was because I was a girl. I know it may seem horrible, but this is what I believed for *many* years!

Yes, I believed the lie. I believed the lie that the father of lies (Satan) placed in that abyss of unanswered questions. This fallacy became my reality and I created a whole framework for managing life and interpersonal relationships based on that one lie.

Over the years, the unanswered questions created a natural curiosity that bordered on insatiable. Like my longing to truly discover why my father left, I had a need to discover the how's and why's about everything. I started taking apart things like the radio, other electronics, and the piano to see the inner workings and discover where the sound originated. My investigations became so bad that my mom threatened severe punishment if I didn't stop. So, I figured out how to take things apart, enjoy my discovery adventure, and then put them back together in their original working condition to avoid any potential punishment. I became naturally wired to figure things out on my own. My mischief then moved from physical objects to liquids and chemicals. I was disassembling, reassembling, or mixing some bizarre, smoke-emitting chemical, at any given time. Then, there were the fires—small kitchen fires, mostly.

Needless to say, it was a stressful time for my mother. The devastation of divorce and a child who had secretly enrolled herself into a "How to be a

Sociopath" self-study course, was nearly too much for her to handle.

Fortunately, being an educator, mom knew exactly how to redirect all of that energy. She had me continue the piano lessons I started earlier, and soon afterwards enrolled me into art school. To top it off, she gave me my first journal and encouraged me to write about the adventures of each day. Any free time I had, my hands were busy with something creative and productive, instead of destructive.

While all of those things were going on at home, school was even more difficult. I was a dark-skinned, chubby girl with glasses. I also didn't speak like the other children, lacking the southern accent, even though I, like most of them was born in North Carolina. I was told I talked weird and "proper". None of that was the packaging required to be a part of the "in crowd". In fact, other children constantly called me "fat, black, and ugly" and other choice names.

I detested having to ride the bus to school. My house was located on one of the last stops on the route. When I got on the bus many of the seats were filled and I was denied access to the few seats that were available. So I'd stand in the aisle or scrunch down near the floor so the bus driver wouldn't fuss at me. I felt humiliated. Nearly every day began the same way—having to face the shameful rejection of neighborhood children on the way to school. Eventually, I decided to walk to another part of the neighborhood to catch the bus earlier in the route and get on before all the seats were filled. Again, I needed to figure out a plan to get through another challenge.

Life continued with other challenges, strained friendships and relationships. All of these issues were based on my skewed perception. I believed that there was a part of me that was simply not good enough. From the very core of my being, I was lacking something that could make me a useful part of anyone else's life or enjoyment. I moved into every setting with one goal and one goal only—to be liked.

About three years after my parents' divorce, my mother's health began to decline and she met a man who became a close friend and helper to her. He was always available to help with household and electrical repairs. He seemed to know now to repair everything; you name it, he could fix it. Most importantly, he did not have any problem at all with me being a girl. In fact, he seemed quite pleased that I was a little girl.

My mother's health continued to worsen and she eventually stopped teaching, went on disability, and began dialysis treatments. As she prepared for these changes, she sent me away to live with family for a few months and when I came back, things were different. This time, there was conversation—not about my father, but about how I needed to be prepared for the way our lives were changing.

"Here are the medicines I will need to take every day. I need you to help me make sure I take these, okay?"

"Yes, ma'am." *I've never seen her so sick.* I thought. *I have to help her, it's just us.*

"Somedays I won't feel too well, so I'll need you to help me take care of more things around the house, okay?"

"Yes, ma'am."

Conversations like these continued as she needed more and more of my help as time went on. The pressure of being a caregiver for my mom as a child was terrifying, but I had to be strong. Seeing her receive dialysis treatments, watching her blood move through the machines and reenter her body, and helping her get into bed or onto the sofa to rest at home after the debilitating sessions were now all a part of our normal lives. There was no time to be a teary-eyed little girl. My mom needed my help and I needed to handle it. I hated seeing her sick, so I stepped up to do as much as I could.

Mom had dialysis treatments three to four times a week. On the weekends I either stayed with her at the dialysis clinic or, for a break, she let me go and spend Saturday mornings with her friend who had become the household handyman.

He lived in a small wood-framed house with a garden on the side yard. I so enjoyed being in the garden. It allowed me to see where some of the vegetables I loved came from. The man gave me gloves and let me dig around in the yard, helping to plant seeds and keep the rows in order. The smell of the rich dirt and plant life were always the best parts of those Saturdays.

Yet fun times in the garden, planting tomatoes and okra, soon became sullied by an older man who had unhealthy intentions with a little girl that just wanted to be liked.

He always called me "Jody". I don't know why he chose to call me that name, but in my family everybody had nicknames. I even had a family nickname, but I was grateful that he liked me enough to give me his very own personal nickname. It made me feel special.

The freedom of idle time, an ill mother, and an unwitting child created too much opportunity for this man's own mischievous curiosities. For the next two years, be privately referred to me as his girlfriend and had sexual intercourse with me nearly every time he "babysat" me while my mother received dialysis treatments. Before I knew it, this was the norm. It just happened so fast.

I never said a word about it to anyone. Once it was over, we continued on with life as if it never happened. The man was still a family friend and came by our home just as frequently as he did before. As far I know, my mother never knew anything about it.

Five years later, my mother passed away. I went to live with other relatives and except for one other occasion I never saw or spoke to the man about the molestation.

❦

Nearly thirty years later, I was entertaining a small group of friends at my home before we left to go hear a local musical group perform. One of the gentlemen, who was formally a stylist, made a few suggestions on how I could update my look.

"You're really attractive, and pretty sexy. If you just wore your hair a little longer, it would take your look to the next level."

"No, I don't know if I should," I responded. "I really don't want people looking at me like that."

"Were you abused?" The question was asked by one of my female friends observing the discussion.

Wow! No one has ever asked me that before now.

"Well, actually, yes. I have been abused." I said.

"Oh my goodness," she replied. "I'm so sorry."

We had a brief conversation about the sexual molestation and I admitted to them that it was the very first time I had ever told anyone about it. I was a little embarrassed that she asked me such a direct question, especially in mixed company. My friends were supportive and I trusted them with the information.

The realization came to me that it had been several years since I had even recalled or thought about that part of my life. Maybe I forgave it and forgot it. Perhaps I suppressed it and thought I had packed it all away, never to be uncovered again. That day, the Holy Spirit caused it to be revealed. Apparently, parts of my life were showing evidence that something needed to be unpacked and properly addressed.

That night I began journaling and recalling the interactions with the family friend. I don't recall how it even started. Whether he touched me first or he asked for me to touch him. I don't remember the details. All I know is that it continued for those two years until one day I informed him that I was "having cycles" and was aware that I could have babies.

He never threatened to harm me or my mother. He never made me feel guilty for him wanting to have sex with me. He never even asked me to keep it secret. He was my friend. He made our "fun times" together special. He was the first man/father-figure that took any interest in me and I like the attention.

If I had questions about what he was doing to me, he answered them in a way that was easy for me to understand. We had conversations and he listened to what I had to say. It wasn't just conversations about sex, but anything; he listened and talked with me. *Being a child in the South at that time, having grown-up conversations with an adult was a rare privilege.* Why would I tell anyone? I enjoyed it.

That was the most overwhelming discovery. *I enjoyed it?* How is it possible for an eight-year-old girl to enjoy having sex with a man in his fifties? When I consider what was enjoyable about the experience, I don't believe it was, by any means an orgasmically pleasurable time. In fact, I definitely remember feeling grossed out by his sweatiness and being uncomfortable with the ways my body responded to him. I recall how his house smelled of moth balls, and the scratchy brown fabric on the sofa in the room where we spent time. Most of the sexual interaction

> Over time, I learned that in order to be liked, I had to have something to offer.

was actually pretty miserable, so it was not the sex that I enjoyed. I derived pleasure from being his "Jody", having access to a special friend that liked me, and being able to talk with him in a way that I could with no one else. What could I have been missing at such an early age that those "special times" with that man could have been anything close to enjoyable?

To put it simply, I enjoyed being liked. I enjoyed receiving from him what I innately needed to receive from my father—time, attention, and acceptance. In addition, my mother was sick then and fighting for her life. She needed help with her daughter and he was the "help" that was available.

By the time my mother passed away, just before my fifteenth birthday, the pieces of the framework were assembled for getting what I needed from relationships. Over time, I learned that in order to be liked, I had to have something to offer. My years of adolescence, college, and young adulthood continued to expand and broaden my framework. Whether it was intellect, money, or my body, I had to have something to trade to get what I needed.

Otherwise, I was going to be left alone, humiliated, and rejected. Just being me was not enough.

Part 2

WHERE'S MY TRIPLE A?

Have you ever been in your vehicle and all of a sudden it gives you trouble? Maybe it makes an unusual noise or it starts shaking in an unfamiliar way. Many years ago, I purchased a car from an ad in a local newspaper. It worked fine for several months, but before long, the problems started. On my way to work one day, the car started to smoke and was losing power. I pulled over onto the shoulder of the highway. The first thing that came to mind was "Oh no! I need to call AAA."

Most of us know AAA, the travel and insurance service, because it represents rescue, safety, and protection. No matter the time of day or night, just give AAA a call and they will come to help you. I didn't have a mobile phone or AAA. Like me, those who don't have AAA have to pull over to the side of the road and depend on the kindness of strangers or convince a friend to stop what they are doing to come and help. Sometimes when we don't have AAA and no friends are available, we just have to WALK.

In life, I found myself in need of another Triple A—Affirmation, Approval, and Acceptance. The need for Affirmation, Approval, and Acceptance can be one of the most motivating forces in our lives. It can display itself in various ways. For some, it may lead to attention-seeking behavior (positive or negative); for others, it can display itself in abusive ways where the emotions of others are manipulated to achieve a desired result through rants and tirades. For me, I was always available to help in my role as "Helpful Holland". By being helpful, I knew people were going to appreciate what I could offer them.

If there was a project team at work or church, I was one of the first ones to volunteer to take on critical tasks. I wanted to be known as the most reliable and resourceful member of the team. I invested countless hours and skills, finances to support the project goals, just to get the verbal and non-verbal recognition for being a valued team member. The "thank you" sentiments, invitations to project meetings, and small gifts of gratitude provided the dosages to fill the craving for Triple A.

The hits of Triple A were potent and toxic. Not that is wrong to desire to help others. The issue is when it is done with the sole desire of receiving the pat on the back and letting that be my source of self-worth. It was just as toxic as a shot of a lethal drug.

Going after Affirmation, Approval, and Acceptance led me to walk into friendships and relationships willingly offering everything and anything I had, just as long as there was even a small potential of getting Triple A. For others, I have foolishly paid rent, bought groceries, driven miles to

> The need for Affirmation, Approval, and Acceptance can be one of the most motivating forces in our lives.

other cities, and committed countless other misuses of my time and money, for the purpose of winning affection and the interest of others—only to find out that the efforts would not be reciprocated or provide the lasting Triple A I desired. I yielded my time, intellect, money, and body for a few pats on the back, moments of time, "thank you" sentiments, and late night return phone calls.

While I walked away with my head held high and a pep in my step, it was only temporary. As soon as that last dosage wore off or I encountered another challenge to my self-esteem, I was right back at it, looking for the next opportunity to "help", all the while needing so much from those who had no real ability to give me anything close to what I truly needed.

I was in a continual cycle. In need of Triple A, I gave all that I could to people just to get a tinge of the feeling of being a meaningful part of someone's life, only to be disappointed that the feeling didn't last. Then I had to find either a new way to give of myself, or just find someone new to get the level of Triple A I wanted. The cycle was ongoing to the point that I no longer had any clue about what was left or who I was. I felt rejected, depleted, betrayed, not good enough, and even hopeless at times—all of it in a futile attempt to get enough Triple A to make up for all of my believed insufficiencies. I had no idea how to get out.

This is a dangerous position to experience, especially if your only sources of Affirmation,

Approval, and Acceptance are external. Every bit of self-worth is quantified and determined by how people respond to you and perceive you. Yet people can be fickle. What they love about you today can be the same thing they despise and dismiss you for tomorrow.

From childhood, I learned about God and attended church over the years. I was taught to fear God and to obey Him or be ready for the awaiting punishment. Even during this period of time of seeking Triple A, there was church attendance and religious activities, but no real relationship with my Creator. I simply had "fire insurance" to keep me out of Hell and failed to allow my relationship with God to become substantial enough to replace the external messaging. I refused to trust God to fill my heart with the internal knowing of the real source of Triple A.

So, I continued. I continued to seek my Affirmation, Approval, and Acceptance from external sources, resulting in years of a depleted self-image, self-hating behavior, dysfunctional relationships, and misused time. Rejection sends us on a mission to seek and destroy our self-esteem. One of the worse aspects of rejection is that, at times, we become the enemy of

☐

our own self-worth. Rejection attacks how much we value ourselves.

The efforts and activities in pursuit of Acceptance, Love, and Belonging, especially when we are combatting rejection in unhealthy ways, will cause us to devalue ourselves and experience situations, relationships, and interactions that further reduce our self-esteem. When we devalue ourselves, there is a willingness to accept situations that align with how we see ourselves. If

> Rejection sends us on a mission to seek and destroy our self-esteem.

you have the choice of the best options but believe that you are not eligible for the best, then you will tend to choose options that are perceived to be more accepting and that you are equipped to support.

We endure these substandard events just to get a little, temporary boost. We find ourselves looking for opportunities to be available for this punishment. The smallest communication or acknowledgment becomes the elixir we seek, hoping this time will last and be more fulfilling. We allow our standards, our self-respect, and our feelings to be trampled and disregarded. Oftentimes, we are simply ignored until the person has a need, then we are more than ready to make ourselves available. In the end, we find ourselves right back where we began. Sometimes even lower.

Part 3

FILLING THE VOID TO AVOID FEELING THE VOID

M any of us have heard the saying that we all
have a "God-sized" void that only God can
fill. Well, I was painfully aware of that void and I did
my absolute best to fill that void and my time with
almost anything that made the presence of that void
less noticeable—well, less noticeable to me, at least.
Again, I was walking in a fog, believing lies and
creating a reality that by no mean was aligned with
the truth.

Yet the more I tried to occupy and silence the
void, the more present it became. The delusional
efforts of trying to placate and pacify the longing that
now refused to be quieted became useless. The
unfilled areas of my life refused to be satisfied with
temporary fixes. What I wished to stifle and sweep
under the proverbial "rug" was now hollering and
acting out in the most inappropriate and
uncomfortable ways. This was painful and

exhausting. I was angry and didn't know how to quiet the echoes of the void. To address that longing called for more strength, honesty, and faith than I thought I was able to muster up—so I continued to fill, rather than feel.

I filled the void with that I call the Three Fs— Fun, Fellas, and Food. The Three Fs were my go to. Whenever there was a time or space where I needed a self-esteem boost, especially during the times when I was missing my Triple A, I knew exactly where to go. If the fun wasn't available, then surely there was a fella to call on. If no fella was at the ready, not to worry—there was always food. The Three Fs represented everything that brought pleasure and euphoria to me. I'd

> The void was vast and it was loud; constantly sending echoes throughout my life of how it needed to be filled.

rather feel this ignorant bliss than feel the void that constantly call out for something real. Ravi Zacharias, renowned Christian author and apologist, is noted for saying, "Pleasure without God, without the sacred boundaries, will actually leave you emptier than before."

This could not be any truer then in my life. These were the sedatives that made the feelings of unworthiness, lack of true connectivity with others, and rejection easier to bear. At times, it even seemed that they did not exist at all. From the outside, most people assumed that I was just a confident person, moving through young adulthood with every hope and advantage that life brings. Little did they know that during the moments when my Triple A was lowest and the Three Fs were hard to acquire, there was depression and thoughts (and attempts) of suicide constantly occupying my life.

The void was wide and deep. The void was vast and it was loud; constantly sending echoes throughout my life of how it needed to be filled. All of my attempts to fill it left me feeling fatigued, but I was afraid to try another approach. So I continued with the superficial relationships and friendships allowing people to hang out and use my resources, intellect, and money, but never allowing them access to who I was on an authentic level.

At times, rejection creates surges of anger and aggression. Rather than show hurt or depression when encountering or expecting rejection, we can display anger and aggression as a defense mechanism. This can produce a perpetual cycle of dysfunction. Typically, people do not want to develop friendships and relationships with people that are angry and aggressive (unless they, too, are angry and aggressive). In most cases, the person who responds with anger and aggression is avoided and therefore, experiences further rejection. Over time, this anger and aggression can develop into bitterness, mean-spiritedness, and relational dysfunction— and it all stems from an attempt to build a "thick skin" and lessen the impact of rejection.

> Unresolved rejection that remains over time begins to impact our bodies in physical ways.

I also continued pursuing romantic relationships that provided time and attention, but devalued everything I was and everything I was made to be. I continued abusing myself by displaying self-hating,

☐

dysfunctional behavior, and allowing myself food addictions to placate emotional issues. I allowed my health to be put at risk and was heading down a road to an early death.

Rejection piggybacks on physical pain pathways in the brain. Unresolved rejection that remains over time begins to impact our bodies in physical ways. The emotions, thoughts, and internal messages that travel through our brains have the ability to produce physiological outcomes, meaning that the way we think about ourselves can create results in our bodies. Consider all of the illnesses caused or worsened by stress, such as migraines, high blood pressure, insomnia, and may more. Often, rejection lies at the root.

I was doing all of this just to avoid dealing with the hole in my heart from a rejection that happened so many years earlier. My life was in limbo. I was empty and unfulfilled. My schedule was full with lots of activity, but I was still living in the void. I was doing a lot and doing nothing at the same time. My purpose was in jeopardy. Surely there had to be more for me.

I had to make a decision. I was sick and tired of being sick and tired for being sick and tired! I wanted more and I knew more was available. I saw it happening in the lives of other people. I knew God loved me just as much as He loved them! I had to find a way to get to it. I had to find a way to get better. I had to WALK out of the void. I had to WALK away from the rejection.

Section 1 – Points to Ponder

1. Take a moment and reflect on your experiences with rejection (no matter how great or small). List them here.
2. When did the first one of these experiences with rejection happen?
3. How has this rejection impacted your life?
4. Do you believe this rejection is still impacting your life in any way? How?

Section 1 – Let's Pray

Heavenly Father, I thank you for giving me an opportunity to think about the experiences I have had in my life. I am grateful that you are present with me as I reflect and are constantly protecting my mind. Thank you for the guidance of your Holy Spirit to help me sift through the memories and provide clarity.

Please help me uncover any hidden places that are necessary for me to experience the true peace and freedom that you have prepared for me. Thank you for healing my broken places and bandaging my wounds. Thank you for embracing me through this process, knowing that there is nothing that I have done or will do that will cause you to stop loving me. I trust you.

In Jesus's Name. Amen.

Section 2

Let's Take the WALK Together

Holland B. Nance

Part 1

BE WILLFUL

...that He would grant you according to the riches of His glory, to be strengthened with might through His Spirit in the inner man. Ephesians 3:16 (NASB)

...do not be conformed to this world, but be transformed by the renewing of your mind,... Romans 12:2 (NASB)

T he first step to taking this WALK toward freedom from rejection is to be WILLFUL. Willful, in this context, can be described as "intentional and deliberate; being headstrong, refusing to change your ideas." This means that we must first make up in our minds that we will no longer accept being trapped by the reigns of rejection.

We must now develop an antagonistic relationship with rejection. It is no longer an excuse for why we haven't achieved, no longer a valid reason to continue to live a life that is less than everything that God has designed for us. We are not victims, we are willfully ready to change our minds, our hearts, and our activities to become overcomers!

Now, I will warn you. This will be tough. Yes, this may even be one of the hardest things you will ever accomplish. Your mind will have to shift to a more focused, strategic, and purposeful position. There has to be an internal boldness and strength to be this fearless in every area of your life. It will take a willful spirit and a willful attitude.

You may ask, "How can I develop this willful attitude to move to this unchartered internal territory?" I'm glad you asked. You have to decide that enough is enough! Enough of living life in a box waiting for others to open it and give you permission to experience everything God has made available to you. Enough of accepting relationships that are far less than reciprocal and enriching. Enough of feeling afraid to pursue your purpose rather than always doing what pleases others. There comes a time when you realize that there is more—but you just don't know how to make this "more" happen. This feeling of "enough" can be just the spark you need to begin being purposeful and intentional about leaving the confines of rejection.

For me, this feeling of "enough" came when I found myself in the depleting cycle of pursuing Triple A without finding fulfilling and lasting results. I loaned, or better yet, gave away plenty of money. I compromised my moral and physical standards by giving myself to relationships that were far less than quality. I took mind-boggling risks and put myself in physical and emotional danger. All of that left me feeling used, abused, and simply dumb for opening myself to those circumstances while truly not experiencing any real benefits.

> We must now develop an antagonistic relationship with rejection.

I grew tired of making bad choices and asking God to rescue me from the consequences of those decisions. The crying, the disappointment, the fear of contracting disease—all of it was exhausting and left me feeling ashamed, guilty, and out of touch with who I really was. I knew I could live better. I knew I could expect better for myself. I knew I could break the cycle of seeking Affirmation, Approval, and

Acceptance from external sources. I knew I could begin nurturing a real relationship with God and allow myself to develop an internal source of Triple A.

The truth of the matter is that we all must realize that we have a wellspring of life that exists within us through our faith in and relationship with Jesus Christ. Unless we tap into this well and draw from it on a consistent basis, we will continue to experience the ongoing thirst and need for the Affirmation, Approval, and Acceptance without the hope to know that we *already have it* within us.

I prayed and asked God to forgive me, heal me, and help me—in those moments when I wanted to revert to my typical methods of seeking Triple A. Help me to know that I can find everything I need in God because He has the ability to fill every one of those voids. Help me to strengthen my mind and my spirit to know that I can finally live a fulfilling life. This understanding and willful commitment are the critical tools that helped me break free from the confinement of rejection and the impact of unresolved rejection.

An Escape Plan

When prison inmates make the decision to escape the correctional facility, they come to the point where they decide the risks of escaping (being captured, injured, or killed) are worth it. Simply reaching the point of freedom is worth the planning and hard work necessary to escape. By no means do I advocate prison inmates escaping and putting themselves and others in danger; however, if your mind is imprisoned by the results of rejection, I do want you to immediately prepare your escape plan. If you have been thinking anything less of yourself than all of the wonderful things God thinks about you, you must escape! When opportunities are presented that will allow you to experience the fullness of life but you demean your eligibility by convincing yourself that you don't deserve it, it is time for you to be released from the confinement that is holding you back. By all means, I want you to escape!

There are risks anytime we commit to making positive changes in life. The first risk may be the possibility that things won't work out as well as we hope. Certainly, when we decide to make improvements, we develop a mental picture of how we imagine our lives will be on the other side of that change. The picturesque views are exciting, encouraging, and motivating. Then reality hits and we discover the process is harder than we thought and the outcomes are not as beautiful as we envisioned. Prepare yourself in advance to enjoy the journey of discovery. Strengthen yourself now for what may lie ahead.

We have to allow ourselves the opportunities that are afforded to us during the process. We will need the endurance to know that it is an ongoing process and with every level, there will be new lessons to learn. The process is risky, but with steadfast commitment, the payoffs are priceless.

Another risk is dealing with others who perceive you differently. People who are used to your typical Triple A gathering style will immediately notice when you stop seeking their Affirmation, Approval, and Acceptance. They will be shocked when that helpful, giving, and compromising person is no longer available and their request is denied with a simple, "No". Indeed, "No" is a complete sentence. People will say that you are changing, and though they said it to demean you; you should take it as a compliment. You *are* changing. You *are* developing. You *are* healing. You *are* escaping!

Lastly, one of the most painful risks is that sometimes you will feel alone. As you being to understand your value and get more in touch with your self-worth, you will not be prone to accept the usual circumstances and people that were previously commonplace in your life. As you lock your mind around escaping, there will be those times where you have to sit in a quiet corner and just observe. Watch for the patterns in the behavior of those who have been a part of your confined life. Notice your feelings about their presence and their absence. Be keenly aware of how life looks for those who are moving freely throughout life without the limitations that you once experienced. This time of observation and introspection will require separation. The separation may, at times, feel like loneliness, but believe me—a willful mindset cannot be exposed to the external influences that may lead it back off course. Begin being comfortable *not* being the one that is constantly called on to help or to be of service. Appreciate the time you gain to make investments in one of the most important people in your life—you.

You must decide that the risks of taking a new approach to life and developing a new mindset about yourself is totally worth it! To begin, develop an unconditional love for yourself. It is important to step back and take a real look at your strengths and weaknesses, your faults and assets, your successes and failures, your wins and losses, and your mistakes and moments of brilliance. Take a real look at all of this and see it for what it is. As you take a moment and appreciate all of the positive parts of your life and examine what part you played in the things that went well, also realize all of the not-so-positive parts and sit in the reality that sometimes you mess things up. It may even be helpful to write these things down in a journal.

Once you have completed this assessment of yourself, your life, your choices, things that have happened that you were responsible for and the things that have happened that you had no control over, then the most important step can take place. Accept it. Yes, accept it. Pray and accept it. Why not? Why wouldn't you accept all that you've been through in life? That's what God did for you. Believe me when I tell you, God accepts you.

You don't believe me? I have proof. Ephesians 1:6 confirms that it is "to the praise of the glory of His grace, by which He made us accepted in the Beloved." (KJV) Yes, He has accepted you. All of the mistakes, the failures, the misgivings, the hurts, the good, the bad, and the very ugly—the holy Creator of the entire universe whose brilliance

> This acceptance does not give you permission to continue to carry out destructive behaviors and to subject yourself to a sub-standard life.

is displayed in the systems that not only hold this world together, but systematically hold you together—He knows you through and through and He still accepts you.

This isn't a decision that He just made about you. He did this back when the world was created. He "has blessed us with every spiritual blessing in the heavenly places in Christ. Just as He chose us in Him before the foundation of the world, that we should be holy and without blame before Him in love." (Ephesians 1:3b-4 KJV) It is the awareness of this love that will fuel the willfulness to truly begin to love yourself and to accept yourself. This acceptance does not give you permission to continue to carry out destructive behaviors and to subject yourself to sub-standard life. Instead, this knowledge should begin to empower you to know that you are worthy of living the life that God has prepared and destined for you. This knowledge should confirm that inner-feeling that has always flitted around your heart that there is a better, a higher, and a more enriching way to live. Now the doors to your freedom are open!

No Second Thoughts, No Backing Out

Consider this. All of the facets of your life have transpired to bring you to the place where you acknowledge how much you matter to God and how much He values you. No matter what has happened and no matter what you have done, He considers you blameless. He doesn't hold any of that against you. He just loves you.

"What about the horrible parts of my life? You mean to tell me that He loves those things? Those things that were done to me that I had no control over or power to prevent? What about those people who should have protected me and shielded me from the evils of this world, who instead offered me up and left me exposed to the worst conditions, the worst situations, and the worst outcomes?"

"What about the emptiness of knowing that someone chose to leave me during the times when I needed them the most? What about the decisions where I knew there were better options, but I chose to do what was convenient?"

"What am I supposed to do with those feelings of anger, disappointment, guilt, and shame that sneak up and tap me on my shoulder to remind me of who and what I am?"

The only answer to these and million other questions like them is to forgive. Forgive others and forgive yourself. This is the next area where the willfulness will be critical. This is where you must realize what stands to be lost in the time spent simmering in the residue of the anger, disappointment, hurt, shame, guilt, and rejection.

Purposefully disassemble the framework that you set up that facilitates your imprisonment. All of that has to be purposefully and intentionally abolished and forgiven in order for you to experience true freedom. Secure your heart and mind today that you have to willfully accept yourself, purposefully forgive those who hurt and disappointed you, and be deliberate about forgiving yourself.

Part 2

ABANDON IT

Bretheren, I do not count myself to have apprehended; but one thing I do, forgetting those things which are behind and reaching forward to those things which are ahead. Philippians 3:13 (KJV)

Loose thyself from the bands of thy neck, O captive daughter of Zion! Isaiah 52:2 (KJV)

Through a series of God-ordained events, I was able to reconnect with my father in 2009. He was eighty years old and sensing that his time on Earth was coming to an end. He was in the hospital's intensive care unit and he wanted to see his children. Despite the nearly twenty-two years that had passed since I had seen him (shortly after my mother's death), I was conflicted about going to see him. I didn't know him. I had no emotional connection with this man with whom I shared so many genetic similarities. My brother, that I was just reunited with around that same time, provided the opportunity to go, so I went. I didn't have any expectations. No list of unanswered questions. All I knew was God had something planned and I wanted to be a part of that plan.

As my brother, his wife, and I journeyed the nine-plus hours from Charlotte, North Carolina to Yonkers, New York, my brother shared information about my father, and it rolled out before me like a never-ending conveyor belt. Story after story. Stories about the family, my father's choices, his relationships, and his activities. Stories of his idiosyncrasies, his preferences, his own disappointments, and his own achievements. When we arrived in New York, I was met by a whole new set of conveyor belts packed with stories shared from the perspectives of former and current wives. Story after story of love relationships, financial decisions, and overall amazement by the reality of the man they married.

Imagine going to a gun range and you are the piece of paper with the outline of the human torso. Let's take it one step further. The gun range is all out of target sheets and you are the last one available. All of the shooters take turns at you. Picture how many holes pierce that thin piece of paper. I felt bombarded.

It seemed everyone that knew him needed to give me information about my father. I didn't have to ask any questions; they volunteered more details than I could ever anticipate.

When we arrived at the hospital, I still saw in my mind that tall, broad, handsome man that I remembered as a little girl. To me, my father could fill a doorway with his stature and fill a room with his personality.

I walked in behind my brother and immediately noticed how small and frail my father appeared in the bed. I listened and smiled as they greeted each other with the familiarity that every father should share with his son. Then my brother announced, "Look who I brought with me!" I smiled big, hoping for that same innate connection.

My father answered, "Is that (giving the name of one of my brother's daughters)?"

"No! I'm not his daughter. I'm *your* daughter." I leaned over onto the hospital bed and gave my father a hug as he called me by my childhood nickname.

I hugged him and smiled politely, but I was angry. I was angry with myself for leaving my home to take that long drive to visit a man who had no clue who I was. Not only did he not recognize me physically, he had no idea who I was as an individual. Who I had become as a young woman. I came all that way to hear all of these stories that created emotions and feelings for a man to whom I had previously been completely numb.

We stayed overnight and left the next day. As we started the drive south, my brother commented on how quiet I was. I knew this was no time for conversation, at least not an external one. I had a lot to process. I ruminated over the stories I heard about my father and the opinions I formulated about him as a result.

I asked God, "Why did You even let me come and be exposed to all of this? Why did You allow me to develop any emotions about my father at all?" Before this trip, I didn't hate him. I wasn't angry with him. I felt nothing concerning my father. Returning home, my heart was filled with resentment and disgust for who my father was. How he used fabrications of truth, manipulations, and selfishness throughout all of his life. I knew these were not the feelings I wanted or needed to carry concerning him.

I wanted to be genuinely able to honor my father in my heart and not feel this anguish about him.

So I prayed. In the midst of my asking "why", I asked the Lord to show me the lessons I needed to learn from this experience. It was obvious that no deep father-daughter relationship was going to blossom from this encounter, so there had to be something more.

During the remaining hours of that trip from Yonkers to Charlotte, I came to the knowledge of a few truths.

The first was that my father's decision to end the marriage with my mother and leave our home had nothing to do with me. It had nothing to do with gender. The fact that I was a little girl was meaningless to the reality of who my father was and his preferences in life. This was a matter completely between my mother and my father. While it affected me, it had nothing at all to do with me. My father left our family because he chose to. It was easier for him to pursue other desires and life objectives in another environment. It was as simple as that.

The second truth was that my mother, like those other wives, wanted something from my father that he just did not have the capacity to give. Despite their beauty, intellect, and resourcefulness, all of them wanted the same thing—to experience authentic love from a gentleman that promised the world. Every person simply wanted to provide and receive a soft and safe place to land. At the end of a day filled with the battles and pressure of life, it is great to have someone to count on to simply be there, but that wasn't the case for them. My father just didn't have the ability to sustain that sort of commitment. Once that place where he was was no longer soft or safe, it was easier for my father to find another soft, safe place rather than fluff and fortify the place he already was.

I abandoned those thoughts of not being good enough, of not being worthy of pure love, and of feeling that I always had to bring something else to the table.

The third truth was that my father and I shared a few personality traits. We both were given the ability to connect with people and make them feel comfortable, sharing their trust with us fairly easily and early in relationships. I now have an acute awareness that this gift of relatability should never be displayed with the purpose of using or manipulating people. I have to be mindful of my personal motivations for every friendships, relationship—and even when I offer to be helpful.

It was over those hundreds of miles where the false realities began to be dismantled. The lies started to shrivel and disintegrate. The reality that the framework I developed as my coping mechanism to gain favor and friendship was the very same thing my father did. I could not sit in that car being angry and judgmental of him when I was guilty of the same thing. So I had to forgive us—both of us.

The second step in taking the WALK to freedom from rejection is to ABANDON any thoughts or residue that stem from a point of rejection. Over those mile, I abandoned those thoughts of not being good enough, of not being worthy of pure love, and of feeling that I always had to bring something else to the table in order for people to feel that I had value. I prayed and asked God to fill those empty spaces that I tried so desperately to fill. I asked Him constantly to make me aware of when I began to shift back into the old habits. I needed God to prick my heart every time I started a relationship or friendship

⏸

with a self-serving purpose and cause me to abort the selfish mission and if necessary, end the relationship or friendship.

What false beliefs do we have that should be abandoned? What defense or coping mechanisms have we set up that we can now shred and toss away? Let's commit now to abandoning every thought about ourselves that support our continuing to live in the confines of rejection.

Part 3

THE BIGGEST LIE

*The heart is more deceitful than all else and is desperately sick;
Who can understand it?* Jeremiah 17:9 (NASB)

Yes, I believed a lie as a child when my parents divorced, but it wasn't the only one. The biggest lie was that for the longest time I believed the reasons for my insecurity, promiscuity, and lack of respect for men all stemmed from my sexual molestation. I thought that was the focus—and it was back in college that I first decided to do something about it.

In my junior year, my school's choir had a concert scheduled at a local church in Charlotte, NC and I thought that would be a good time to confront the man who called me "Jody". I called him; there are some things you never forget like your childhood home address. In this case, it was his phone number. We spoke briefly, catching up on life occurrences over the past decade as though we were long lost buddies, and I invited him to the concert. On the drive over to the church, I scripted in my mind how the conversation was going to take place.

"What were you thinking to have done such a horrible thing to a little girl? I trusted you and that is what you chose to do?"

"I know. I was wrong. I've felt so guilty about it. All of these years I have been miserable, thinking of the ways I hurt you. I'm so sorry. Please forgive me!"

I had it all mapped out. I was going to take the nearly seventy-year-old man to task for his inappropriate behavior. He was going to beg feebly for forgiveness in tears, offering the sincerest apologies. *Yes,* I thought. *I'm not going to let him get away with this!*

As we began singing, my eyes filtered through the many faces in the congregation. With each song, I allowed the tension of the expected confrontation to ease. As I continued scanning the audience between songs, not seeing his face among the crowd caused me to relax and let the inspiring melodies of the music pour peace into my heart and mind. It was the distraction I needed; somewhere deep within I knew I wasn't looking forward to seeing him and having such a critical conversation, especially in this sacred space. I breathed easier.

Later in the concert, though, I spied a gray-haired man entering the sanctuary. I recognized the brown fedora he held in his hand. He quickly took a seat in one of the last few rows. Our eyes met instantly. He nodded and smiled. My body tightened and I was angry. I huffed internally. *I can't even believe he showed up!*

The concert ended and I exited the choir loft. As we walked toward each other, I began sifting through my rehearsed questions and readied myself to sling each one at him as soon as we finished with the standard courtesies. Everything in me wanted to holler and rant, but that would defy my upbringing to be respectful in public with an older adult. We were in a church, after all, surrounded by many of my college friends. I had to handle this carefully.

As I came close to him, he threw his arms open and hugged me. "There's my Jody!" he said happily, as he kissed me on the cheek. "How's my girlfriend?"

I looked straight at him, dumbfounded. I could not believe what had just happened. *Did he just refer to me by the name he gave me while he subjected me to sexual abuse—right here in this church?* It had been nearly eleven years. *Why is he still calling me his girlfriend? This man is sick!*

Then I understood, *Oh my God. He really doesn't see anything wrong with what he did!*

With that realization, my angst was replaced by a flood of sorrow for how sick he actually was. To him, nothing about the relationship was unhealthy. Even worse, in his mind, nothing had changed. There was no longer any need for me to seek revenge or even vindication.

> Life has taught me that you have to grant forgiveness to those who may not or can never request it.

There was no need to press him to realize something for which he had no awareness. I didn't have the energy; and I didn't want to become belligerent and cause a scene. It wasn't worth it. He was simply too sick for even a fake apology from him to be useful to me.

I was done. "It was good seeing you," I said in dismissal. "I have to go now. Our bus will be leaving soon to head back to the campus."

He hugged me again. His embrace made my skin crawl. I kindly tucked my questions back into my soul and walked away. Those questions stayed there for the next twenty years.

Let's pause a moment and understand that I did not give the man who molested me a free pass, nor is it my responsibility to hold him accountable for his life. He passed away in 2008, and he and I never spoke or saw each other after that concert. I know that God has confronted him about the actions and choices he made while here on this Earth. He now has the remainder of eternity to reap any consequences or enjoy any rewards that God has appointed to him. I have forgiven him. It took time, quite a bit of effort, and a lot of prayer to get to that place of forgiveness and closure. I returned to the site where the molestation took place. The home was gone, but a close friend and I went there and prayed on the grounds to eradicate any residual anger, hatred, and need for revenge that remained. Life has taught me that you have to grant forgiveness to those who may not or can never request it.

Trying to Gather the Pieces

During this process, I spent countless hours talking with counselors and ministers discussing the fact that I was a victim of childhood sexual abuse. I also spent unknown amounts of time making links to all sorts of behaviors and decisions based on that two-year period and the subsequent meeting eleven years later. Every time I watched a talk show where there was a person with a similar story or when the host would interview child sex abusers, I wanted to understand as much as possible about how it causes so many dysfunctions in life and relationships. I was trying to saturate my intellect with information so I could finally get to a resolution for the feelings of not being good enough and the constant need to overcompensate, just to fit in.

I read, studied, and continued going to counseling. We discussed and prayed; prayed and discussed and I went right back and repeated the same unhealthy relational behaviors, to being "Helpful Holland" for the wrong reasons. I continued to foster meaningless romantic relationships lacking reciprocity. I still felt horrible about who I was. Why wasn't any of this working?

It wasn't working because I never addressed the underlying issue that began well before the sexual molestation ever took place. This man and the molestation were *not* the focus or the core issue of rejection I experienced. He was simply a pawn to inappropriately distract my healing process. The counseling was necessary and beneficial. It helped me move to the place of forgiveness. The issue is that I focused the counseling on a symptom and worked to fix the symptom without addressing the cause of the symptom. The time I spent in counseling and personal research trying to understand the mind of a molester was useful for many reasons, but it did not provide the resources necessary to help me move forward from the behavior that was debilitating my emotional and spiritual progression. That time could have been more

⁉

effectively used understanding how powerful and lasting the spirit of rejection can be.

I had to ask myself some serious questions. The main one was, "Why did I enjoy the 'special time' with the man that abused me?" Was the experience really enjoyable or was it the time and attention received during the experience that made it appealing? This process led me to discover the real issue. Rejection was the actual root cause.

> We expend countless days, weeks, months, and years battling a mirage.

Rejection was the reason for the need to be liked. Rejection was the creator of the framework for managing life and interpersonal relationships. Rejection was the reason for the insecurity, promiscuity, and the issues with respecting men. Rejection—it was in this revelation where the healing began.

Bishop Kenneth Ulmer states, "One strategy of the devil is to have us go to war against the wrong enemy and on the wrong battlefield." I encountered pain on a daily basis, but kept losing in the process of discovering the cause, all because I was battling the wrong enemy. The father of lies, the devil, uses the strategy of smoke of mirrors to distort our view. We begin responding to what we think we see and shift our focus to fighting against a false depiction. We expend countless days, weeks, months, and years battling a mirage. It consumes our energy, our focus, and delays us from reaching our purpose. This lie existed specifically to steal my power to identify the real cause and quickly move forward to experience all that God has prepared for me. Therefore, time was misused trying to resolve a symptom and delayed addressing the root and core of my issues.

Once I began to dig deeper and realized the core issue, the biggest lie was officially deflated and my focus shifted to resolving the real issue at heart.

Many of us have experienced rejection in the early stages in life. In the midst of this rejection, there is usually a lie that we either developed on our own or a lie told to us about a scenario or ourselves that we believe and hold on to for the remaining years.

Rejection has debilitating effects because it typically causes us to see ourselves with a distorted lens. Based on this distorted view, we develop a plan for dealing with social, professional, and personal environments, interpersonal relationships, and most importantly, our relationship with ourselves.

If you view yourself from a position of insufficiency, you typically enter every opportunity from the perspective that you either have something to prove or from the standpoint that you are disadvantaged and are less than qualified for that opportunity. This false viewpoint can cause you to be in an uncomfortable position. Feeling that you must prove your worth in every scenario, you may be tempted to over-achieve or to be overly-competitive. It may impact your ability to relate cohesively with others, seeing them as a danger to your ability to show your worth. Rather than being able to maximize the collaborative assistance others can provide, you see them as threats and fear they will misuse your resources and eventually take credit and recognition that you are trying to achieve.

In the same way, entering an opportunity from a position of disadvantage can be limiting to your ability to fully experience life. Feelings of insufficiency cause you to hide yourself, your skills, and your openness to friendships and relationships. This pattern of closing yourself off is a defense mechanism to avoid potential rejection. Typically, because the impact of previously experienced rejection has caused social pain and anxiety, you may believe that it is easier to simply not engage and not make yourself available to receive any further disappointment in this way. In essence, you reject others before they have the opportunity to reject you. The danger here is that there are many aspects of life that you are allowing to pass you by—the negative ones and the positive ones.

We can relive and re-experience social pain more vividly than we can physical pain. Social anxiety, social avoidance, and rejection sensitivity are all results of unresolved rejection. Even more, these issues can develop deficiencies in our ability to achieve and sustain healthy relationships—family, social, and romantic. Feelings of not fitting in and of being ostracized and discarded, if not properly addressed, can lead to low self-esteem, and feelings of low self-worth. The pain of experiencing social rejection can be so intense that it creates extreme anxiety.

The only way to rid our lives of this social avoidance and the need to prove our worth to others is to dig deep to find the root of the lie that makes us respond and relate to life with this distorted perspective. It is only when we identify the initial lie that we can begin to dismantle the rejection and the misinterpretation. All of the other efforts will prove to be time-consuming, while yielding temporary results.

Be aware, though, finding the lie may take effort. It may begin by recalling the first time you experienced rejection, that feeling of being insufficient, not good enough, or even left out. Ask yourself about that time and place in your life. How did it feel? Who was involved? Did you make changes to try to get a different result? Have you continued any of this behavior throughout life?

Consider how your life has been impacted by the effects of the lie or series of lies. What about those lies have become truth for you? Think about how life may have been different if you were able to identify the lie earlier in life and WALK in the real truth.

Part 4
KNOW THE TRUTH

You will know the truth, and the truth will make you free. John 8:32 (NASB)

To the praise of the glory of his grace, wherein he hath made us accepted in the beloved. Ephesians 1:6 (KJV)

T o know the truth is the most powerful and critical part of the journey of WALKing from rejection to freedom. It's not easy—because truth itself seems to be evolving into obscurity. I can recall a time when the idea of absolute truth was clear and well established. Now truth seems to be more of an abstract than ever before. Instead of absolute truth, there is experiential truth that prevails as well as the increasingly popular notion of "my truth" that stems from each person taking a viewpoint on a matter and declaring it as truth without any foundational basis. We make major decisions and lifestyle choices based on this unsubstantiated truth. The truth has come to the point of being flexible and convenient.

Years ago, "my truth" was that I was a chubby, dark-skinned daughter of a man who didn't love me because I was a girl. I was not good enough to be genuinely liked or appreciated unless I had something to offer or exchange. This was proven to be the case beginning when I was sexually molested as a child and this was my basis for my interpersonal relationship framework. That was "my truth" for many years, but it had nothing to do with the truth of who I really was, or of who God created me to be.

There are now so many perceptions of what truth is that is almost seems strategic. In fact, I know it is. Ephesians chapter 6 describes the process of preparing and equipping ourselves to stand against the attacks of the enemy of our souls. The second half of the chapter empowers us to "put on the whole armor of God." The list of armor pieces begins in verse 14 with the most essential piece, "stand firm then with the belt of truth buckled around your waist." (NIV)

As I studied this verse and the elements of a suit of armor, I discovered a phenomenally important fact. The armor cannot be held together well without the waistband being securely in place. This piece holds all of the other pieces of the suit together. Secondly, having the waistband fastened firmly provides strength and durability to the frame of the suit.

In this analogy, all of the protection, coverage, and defense we need to withstand the numerous attacks of the devil begins with truth. Now, I understand why truth is challenged from every direction. If truth is not in its appropriate place and used in its most effective way, then our entire frame of strength and endurance is in jeopardy. Our state of mind and our whole existence can be at risk of total annihilation. Our enemy, the devil, wants our minds and thoughts to be riddled continually with confusion and uncertainty. The less truth we know, the less power we have to fulfill our purpose. This is especially true when we are fighting in the battle against rejection.

The challenge is if we define the truth based on our perspective, how can we stand firmly on or securely fasten ourselves to a truth with no foundation—a truth that constantly changes? Isaiah 40:8 provides the answer we need: "The grass withers, the flower fades, But the Word of our God stands forever." (NASB)

God, in His infinite wisdom, is very much aware of the current challenge with the state of truth. He knows how truth is clouded with varying points of view that change as our perspective and viewpoint changes. The Word of God is absolute truth and His thoughts are certain and do not change based on circumstances, the era, or the current events of our day.

Jesus provides a wonderful example of the importance of truth when we are combating lies. The Spirit of God led Jesus into the wilderness without food, for forty days. The devil tempted Jesus by promising to give Him power and authority if Jesus would worship him. The devil wanted Jesus to agree with his proposal.

Rather than reply with an emotional rant about the absurdity of the devil's offer or point out that the devil was offering something that he didn't own, Jesus simply replied, "It is written" and stated the truth of the Word of God concerning each of the devil's proposals. The truth allowed Jesus calmly to dismiss the devil's requests and stand on the power of God's Word. The devil stopped tempting Jesus and left Him. Jesus was able to continue focusing on starting ministry and fulfilling His purpose.

Our responsibility is to take hold of the truth, the Word of God, by faith and let it be the essential piece of our understanding. We must allow what God says to hold us together and fortify us when we are combating the lies and rejections that we encounter in life. The more we expose ourselves to the truth, the more we can understand the truth and develop an attitude of knowing.

This attitude of knowing indicates knowing it in your heart. Proverbs 23:7 reminds us that as a person thinks in his heart so is he (*paraphrased* KJV). This thinking in the heart goes beyond positive affirmations that remind us of the possibilities life has available to us. Those are fine, but if they never reach your heart, the are no more useful than recitations of the names in your phone's contact list.

> If truth is not in its appropriate place and used in its most effective way, then our entire frame of strength and endurance is in jeopardy.

The process of allowing truth to saturate your heart begins with a mental decision. In Section 2, Part 1, I discuss the willful mindset necessary to begin moving toward all that life has available to us. This willfulness is critical to escaping rejection and the various ways it keeps us confined mentally and spiritually. There is a place where we decide that no matter the risks, it is worth it. In this case, the truth is the tool we need to escape. The truth is the pick and the shovel that will help us dig through all the layers that have kept us captive and cramped. The truth is instrumental in progressive movement along the journey to freedom.

With all of this understanding in place, the next step is to determine how do we begin to replace the lies and establish and know the truth? We must be dedicated to finding the truth, believing the truth, and knowing the truth.

Confronted with Truth

A few years ago, I was working with a friend on a professional development project. Since we were both Christians, we thought it would be useful to hold each other accountable for Scripture memorization as a part of the development process. We decided to start with Ephesians chapter 1. During each weekly check in call, we recited a verse beginning with the first verse and with each successive week we added the following verse. Between the calls, I rehearsed the verses and asked God for insight on the Scripture to help me not only memorize it, but understand how it applies to my life.

Early into this process of memorization, the verses began to speak like and empowerment to me. Verses 4-6 state, "According as he hath chosen us in him before the foundation of the world, that we should be holy and without blame before him in love. Having predestinated us unto the adoption of children by Jesus Christ to himself, according to the good pleasure of his will, To the praise of the glory of his grace, wherein he hath made us accepted in the beloved."

Even though I was working to expand an area of my business, I was absolutely undergoing a spiritual and emotional development process, as well. During this time, I was still dealing with unanswered questions from my childhood and the ways that I had coped and answered them as an adult. I developed questions about why my mother chose the men that she did—the one she married and the one she allowed to babysit me. Since I didn't have any way of asking her, I developed my own answers. Along with those answers came judgment against my mother and I blamed her. I could not have been more wrong.

When I read verse 4 and was assured that I was chosen before the world was formed and that I was blameless in His eyes, I was excited to think that a holy, righteous God, that created the whole world and all of the universe chose me. *Wow! Better yet, despite all of the crazy choices and decisions that I have made, He doesn't blame me? Woo Hoo!*

But wait—if I'm blameless, then certainly my mother, my father, and the man that babysat me are blameless, too. How can I blame and hold something against them when God doesn't? I immediately had to repent and ask God to forgive me for holding on to so much anger and resentment. That day, I forgave them all. That was the beginning of realizing the truth of God's love for me; I don't ever have to walk in shame or guilt about anything. Nor do I have the right to hold anyone else in shame or guilt.

> Once we come to the place of knowing the truth, our need for striving, proving, and getting people to affirm our value ceases.

I continued reading and came to verse 6. The truth of God's Word leapt off the page. "I'm accepted." At that moment, I realized that God accepted me!

The inner thoughts that remind us the past instances of rejection, the devastation of heartbreak, and the cycles of disappointment have to be replaced with other thoughts. Not just a thought, but a knowing of what really is truth.

There is a supreme difference in the power of a thought that becomes a knowing that develops into a belief. Those beliefs then grow into habits that shape the direction and course of our lives. The thought process is critical. We have to feed our minds with the proper material that will allow us to elevate and lift our way of thinking about the world, about others, and especially about ourselves.

Once we come to the place of knowing the truth, our need for striving, proving, and getting people to affirm our value ceases. When trying to prove our worth, we spend countless hours, days, months, and years extending ourselves to others, hoping they will finally recognize our worth. We go into thousands of dollars of debt trying to achieve affirmation through acquiring education and material assets. We have children and stay in dysfunctional relationships, all because we have not come to the place of fully knowing the truth about who we are and who God made us to be.

How Do I Know?

The process of knowing the truth can be segmented into three phases. The first is to know your Creator and what He says about you. Based on your understanding of your Creator, you begin to have a better understanding and knowledge of your worth. Lastly, in order to maximize your worth fully, you must know your purpose.

Know Your Creator

God, our creator, is so vast and awesome that I could spend the rest of my days describing His attributes and characteristics, especially as it relates to His ability to be touched and concerned about our issues and needs. Even more, He is able and willing to come to our rescue, as it relates to rejection.

There are three characteristics that are specifically important for us to know as we WALK the journey from rejection to freedom. The first is to understand and know His omnipresence. This means that God is everywhere, at the same time. No matter where you are, God is there. Psalm 139:7-10 reminds us, "Where can I go from your Spirit? Or where can I flee from your presence? If I ascend to heaven, you are there! If I make my bed in Sheol, behold, you are there! If I take the wings of the dawn and dwell in the remotest parts of the sea, even there your hand shall lead me, and your right hand will lay hold of me." (NASB) This is vital for those of us who have suffered the impact of rejection. Among other things, rejection makes us feel alone and isolated. To know that your Creator is there wherever you are or whatever you are dealing with, provides the assurance and hope needed to begin the journey of healing.

The second characteristic to know is His omniscience. God is all-knowing and understands all things, even our most privately held secrets and feelings that reside deep in our hearts. First John 3:20 says, "Even if we feel guilty, God is greater than our feelings, and he knows everything." (NLT) Understanding that there is nothing we can hide from Him can be an unnerving realization, but we have to look at this from a position of peace instead of judgment. He is our Creator and knows every fiber of our being. Why wouldn't He be concerned about our most intimate thoughts and feelings? The beauty is that He knows all of it and loves us, not in spite of us, but because He made us. More importantly, He has the answers we need to move forward.

We often make mistakes in our response to rejection. Whether it's in our approach to new environments or new people, or in the concessions we make to be liked or accepted by others, sometimes we get it wrong. Knowing the omniscience of God helps us understand that nothing we face is beyond His empathy and if we ask Him, He will help us learn, grow, and have a better response the next time we face rejection.

The third characteristic to know is His omnipotence. God is all-powerful. Luke 1:37 says, "For nothing will be impossible with God." (NASB) Life comes with its own set of challenges and issues. If we sat down and listed every obstacle that life has presented, that list could easily fill a page. The blessing is that, while the challenge may have been difficult and painful, you have survived! It is empowering to know there is nothing that can happen in life that is too complex for God to handle. We have to seek His instruction, put our faith in Him and trust in Him to guide us through every situation. One of my favorite scriptures is Romans 8:28. "And we know that all things work together for good to them that love God, to them who are called according to His purpose." (KJV)

Awareness is key for knowing each of these characteristics. I challenge you to become more aware of His presence, understanding, and power in your individual life—on a daily basis—moment by moment. Let this awareness permeate your thought process. Let it guide your activities and choices throughout the day. With this awareness, depressive and suicidal thoughts have to evacuate the corners of your mind. With this awareness, debilitating and destructive relationships are severed. With this awareness, hope, truth, and freedom from rejection will become more tangible than ever before.

Know Yourself and Your Worth

Years ago, I was visiting an art gallery enjoying a few new exhibits and sculptures on display. There was one piece that captured my attention. I stood in front of the object for quite some time, turning my head from side to side and walking around the stand to get different vantage points. The object was a combination of curved and rounded pieces of clay. I wanted to define it and purposed to understand the piece and be able to walk away knowing what it was.

As I continued gazing at the sculpted anomaly, I heard a voice over my shoulder ask, "What do you think this piece is saying?" I turned and responded, spouting a reference to neo-classical art and correlating the weird and confusing shapes to the complexity of life. He smiled, extended his hand, and introduced himself. As soon as he said his name, I wanted access to the secret escape hatch in the floor.

He was the sculptor and my initial comments were less than complementary. I confessed that I was intrigued and challenged by the piece and asked him what he intended for it to say. As soon as he explained his thoughts about the work, it became clear to me. What I stood there earlier trying to define within my limited understanding, now made perfect sense.

The same is true for us. Rather than spending years making valiant efforts trying to define ourselves, why not ask the one who made us? Ephesians 2:10 describes us a God's workmanship. When I think of this term, I consider the detailed craftsmanship of someone who makes carved wooden chairs. The piece starts out as one huge portion of wood. As the artist chisels and chips away each small particle of wood, the form soon starts to take shape. The intricate work continues and after some time, the form begins to look more like the finished product. Once the shape is achieved, then the smoothing and refining process takes place. The artist rubs sandpaper over the wood. As the gritty surface brushes over the wood, the splinters and sharp edges yield to the process and become even and flat. The final step is to paint and seal the wood so that it is protected and reflects the beauty of its unique details.

This is how we should see ourselves. We are not here by happenstance. We are handcrafted creations. Psalm 139:14 reminds us that we are "Fearfully and wonderfully made: your (God's) works are wonderful." (NIV)

Our Creator was very intentional about us. He has a plan for our lives and once we begin to know more about our Creator and allow this awareness to saturate our total being, we can truly lock in on who we are and how much value God places on each one of us.

If you are looking for a guide in understanding your value to God, utilize the tools found in the companion workbook to assist you as you continue your journey.

Know Your Purpose

Since we know that God is intentional about what He has made, then we know that each of us has a purpose for being alive and surviving all that we have encountered through life. Yes, we all have the purpose of worshiping God and bringing praise to Him. Ephesians 2:10 states, "For we are His workmanship, created in Christ Jesus for good works,

⸮

which God prepared beforehand so that we would walk in them." (NASB) In addition, we each have individual assignments to fulfill while we are here on the Earth.

In the same way that we ask our Creator about who we are, we should ask Him about our purpose. A great place to start is to ask Him about the pain, life events, and passions that we have experienced. One frequent question to consider when discovering purpose is, "What problem in the world would I fix if I could?" This often points to our purpose.

Some may be challenged with the idea that God would even entrust them with a purpose. Just know that no matter the distractions and how busy life may become, "Many are the plans in a person's heart, but it is the Lord's purpose that prevails" (Proverbs 19:21 NIV). Others may consider because of past decisions and mistakes, God may have changed His mind or may be angry with them regarding their purpose. Psalm 103:9 assures us, "He will not constantly accuse us, nor remain angry forever." (NLT)

No matter what the challenge may be, know that every day that we exist is an opportunity for us to see the vision, purpose, and plan for our lives to unfold more clearly. The objective is to identify the purpose and begin living in that purpose in the most consistent and productive way. Just remember God is always there to strengthen and empower you along the journey.

Before He Said, "Let There Be," He Knew You Would Be

Genesis 1 describes the creation of the heavens and the Earth. Each day God spoke, "Let there be," and the objects and beings began to exist. On days one through five, He reviewed His creations and "saw it was good." When we look at creation, the remarkable thing is that on the sixth day, God decided to make mankind in His own image. He created male and female and gave specific instructions for how they were to maintain everything else that was created. Once that was completed, He looked over everything and saw that is was "very good."

Many of us are lovers of nature and have a deep appreciation for all of the beauty and majesty of God's creations. While in God's assessment those things were good, they pale in comparison to His creation of us. In His own words, He rated us higher than all of the other creations. Ephesians 1:4 says,

"For he chose us in him before the creation of the world to be holy and blameless in his sight, in love." (NIV)

It makes my heart glad to know that when all of creation was being made, He had you in mind. No matter the challenges, disappointments, heartbreaks, bad decisions, or losses; to Him, you are highly rated. You are chosen, blameless, and accepted!

Section 2 – Points to Ponder

1. Take a moment and reflect on what you are willing to have a willful attitude about.

2. What are you willing to do to experience freedom from rejection, whether or not anyone agrees and participates with you?

3. What debilitating thoughts or ideas about yourself and your life are you willing to abandon?

4. What lie(s) have you believed?

5. How has deception impacted your life?

6. What do you know about God, your worth, and your purpose that you haven't considered before?

Section 2– Let's Pray

Heavenly Father, I thank you for empowering me to begin to WALK this journey. I invite you and your presence to accompany me as I continue to move forward. Father, help me to be aware that you are here right along with me. You know everything that I am going through as you are peeling away the layers of pain and smoothing out all of my rough places. Thank you for healing me and constantly encouraging me to do more than I ever thought was possible. Thank you

[?]

for guarding my heart and my mind from depression and suicidal thoughts. I appreciate how much you love me and I am grateful for the gift of salvation. Father, you are all-powerful, all-knowing, and always here with me. I trust you.

In Jesus's Name. Amen.

Section 3

WALK or BEND

Holland B. Nance

Part 1

SO MUCH IS AT STAKE

Today I have given you the choice between life and death, between blessings and curses. Now I call on heaven and earth to witness the choice you make. Oh, that you would choose life, so that you and your descendants might live! Deuteronomy 30:19 (NLT)

That no advantage may be gained over us by Satan; for we are not ignorant of his devices. 2 Corinthians 2:11 (ASV)

For I know what I have planned for you, says the LORD. I have plans to prosper you, not to harm you. I have plans to give you a future filled with hope. Jeremiah 29:11 (NET)

E very day you make choices. You decide what to wear, what to eat, and what route to take on the way to work. Sometimes you get so accustomed to making the same choices over and over that they become habits. Before you know it, there are times when you are going through the motions completely on autopilot. At times, you are not even aware of how you got to work. You look up and you're there;

driving into the parking lot. Your mind is completely disconnected from the process.

Even more, it is not just the daily tasks that become unconscious functions, but unresolved rejection can have an involuntary impact on how you view life, relationships, and opportunities. You can decide to continue to move through life in a less-advantageous position or you can be empowered to be a co-laborer with God in fulfilling all that you were created to accomplish. Please know this decision will have life-changing consequences.

As a reminder, we all have a purpose—the reason why we exist. Whether you have come to realize what that purpose is or not, it does not remove the fact that you have one. Rejection, simply put, it the worst enemy to your purpose.

Rejection destabilized our need to belong and leads to lack of fulfillment. Abraham Maslow developed what is known as "Maslow's Hierarchy of Needs". In this hierarchy, there are five levels of needs. Right at the center (Stage Three) is the need for Love and Belonging. Love and Belonging is where we develop and fulfill the needs for Acceptance, Friendship, Intimacy, and Family. This is where the need for Triple A resides. Maslow's theory notes if any of these stages are not achieved, we cannot be motivated to move forward to pursue the next and higher stage. The highest stage of need (Stage Five) is the need for Self-Actualization—the realization and fulfillment of our greatest potential or our purpose. As long as rejection is unresolved, an unrealized purpose is at risk.

Unresolved rejection creates fear, fosters a diminished outlook about our ability to accomplish desired objectives, and it develops into what equates to an atmosphere of confinement. All of this leads to us being caught in cycles of trying to satisfy our need for love and belonging in artificial and insufficient ways. When we find ourselves bogged down with these efforts, the elevated thinking of identifying, pursuing, and achieving our God-given purpose is frequently pushed to a lower priority. We are busy pursuing and supporting dysfunctional relationships with family, friends, and romantic interests without the proper tools to develop these relationships into healthier and more rewarding experiences. We create internal plans of what we will acquire and accomplish for the sole purpose of proving our worth without truly acknowledging and understanding that our intrinsic value is great whether we ever achieve those things or not.

There is a lot at stake here, but the powerful news is we have a choice. We can decide to WALK the Truth (Willfully Abandon Lies and Know the Truth) or BEND (Believe Every Negative Device) from the enemy. It is easy to stay in the doldrums of the familiarity of what we are used to enduring. The fear and the resistance of that has to be overpowered will take every possible bit of our willful attitude to begin to maximize this life-changing opportunity. When we make the choice to WALK the Truth, we literally make the choice to alter the trajectory of our lives and begin to broaden the scope of our possibilities. We have the power to step out of the cycles and begin WALKing toward the freedom that awaits.

As we consider the choices that lie before us, we should fully understand all of the options. Our goal is to understand, as 2 Corinthians 2:11 states, "that no advantage may be gained over us by Satan; for we are not ignorant of his devices." (ERV) The choice to BEND (Believe Every Negative Device) is a difficult position to take, but many of us find ourselves subjected to these devices as a part of our normal way of life. There are many devices that are used by the enemy of our souls, but we will focus on the seven that most directly impact our ability to properly resolve rejection and therefore places fulfilling our purpose in grave danger.

Part 2

BE AWARE
OF THE DEVICES

1. *Discord and Unforgiveness*

a. In the list of the things God hates found in Proverbs 6:16-19, the seventh one listed and the one that disgusts God the most is "he that sows discord." When God views something so strongly, it is imperative that we fully understand how this device can be disruptive and detrimental to our lives. Discord is the conflict that is stirred up to create friction, hostility, and disagreements between people. Oftentimes the inability to forgive offenses and past disagreements is the sources of the need for creating discord.

b. Discord is so dangerous because when we are constantly seeking to cause strife, we lose the ability to see one another as agents of collaboration. Rather than seeing others as partners along the shared journey of life, enabled with the skills and influence to mutually help one another, they are seen as competition and threats to our ability to move forward. The scheme of the enemy is to envelop our lives with relationships full of this strife and conflict, which eventually lead to divisions and isolations. We end up feeling emotionally alone, dejected, and miss one of the biggest blessings in this life—healthy and fruitful relationships.

2. *Distractions*

a. The device of distractions is broad and can encompass various aspects of life. We can be distracted by striving to prove ourselves, acquire needless material objects, pursuing superficial relationships, and gaining achievements to show others how valuable we are. The efforts it takes to position ourselves in the right place at the right time so we can rub elbows with the right people can pull us away from more intrinsically beneficial activities. The parable in Luke 8:14 describes the seed (the Word of God) that falls onto thorny ground is choked out by life's worries, riches, and pleasures—so that the seed never matures. Distractions are the issues of life that occur and fill our minds and hearts with interferences.

b. A life riddled with distractions is spent scurrying from one moment of crisis to the next. The enemy causes our hearts to be ever in pursuit of resolving issues, planning strategies to position ourselves, and focusing on resolving symptoms rather than addressing the need of knowing our self-worth and building our self-image in Christ.

3. *Disappointment*

a. Life sometimes seems to be rampant with the device of disappointment. When our hopes and expectations are not carried out in the way we imagine, we feel let down, sad, and dismayed. Dr. Randy Carlson, psychologist and author, uses this formula: expectations *minus* reality *equals* disappointment. These frequent unmet expectations may lead to feelings of depression and self-loathing. Proverbs 13:12 informs us that "hope deferred makes the heart sick, but desire fulfilled is a tree of life." (NIV) Over time, disappointment causes us to be distrusting and resist the openness required for fruitful relationships. In other cases, continuous hoping without strengthening our ability to learn after disappointments develops into a life filled with naïve decisions that result in us feeling depleted.

b. Disappointment is a heartbreaking device because it leads to resentment and feelings of isolation. When we feel alone in life, the enemy can then whisper lies to us about ourselves and about how people perceive us. Any time we make decisions based on a lie, we are tracking in the wrong direction. Actually, every disappointment is an opportunity to learn more about ourselves. We can gain better understanding of how to manage and cope with future disappointments in the most positive way.

4. *Discouragement*

a. The device of discouragement is a crafty tool of the enemy. This draining device focuses on zapping the enthusiasm and inspiration out of life, so much so we don't want to try anymore. This feeling of defeat directly influences our confidence and causes us to miss opportunities when we attempt to avoid expected disapproval. Rejection and discouragement go hand-in-hand. Once rejections occurs, the feelings of resentment and the impacts of the offense are soon to follow.

b. Repeated discouragement can create such negative thoughts about ourselves and our surroundings that life can see too difficult to manage. Rather than being sucked into this abyss of pessimism, we have to follow the example given by David in I Samuel 30:6 and encourage ourselves. Realizing that it is not of any special power that we have within ourselves that makes us effective, but the sustaining grace of God that empowers us to achieve. With his knowledge, we can overcome the device of discouragement.

5. *Deceit and Dishonesty*

   a. The devil, often referred to as the "father of lies" (John 8:44) (NIV), is skilled at the art of smoke and mirrors. The device of deceit is typically the portrayal of one thing that leaves the underlying truth to be revealed much later. The misrepresentation of truth is a critical devices used to create powerlessness for one and control for the other. Deceit also allows one to gain an advantage over another, resulting in soul-wrenching pain once the truth is fully known. Even worse is the temptation to become deceptive to manipulate outcomes in your favor. Many who have been rejected fall into this trap as a defense mechanism to avoid future recurrences. Even if they are rejected, they feel that they have leveraged the opportunity without truly opening themselves, so to them, the loss is minimal.

b. The biggest loss experienced by those who use the device of deceit and dishonesty is that their integrity is corrupted. They determine it is easier to continue in this behavior rather than invest the time in building character and regaining the trust of others. Over time, this is a very lonely and bitter life to live. The practice of trying to "get" someone before they have the chance to discover your real intent is a life that lacks true, authentic love and profoundly enriched relationships with others.

6. *Double-mindedness*

a. The device of double-mindedness means literally to have two minds. In one instance you believe one thing, but in another instance you do the opposite. You make choices based on what is more beneficial to you or what the greater influence over your choices would be. The restlessness and confusion associated with this way of thinking and living creates a life of inconsistency. James 1:8 tells us, "a double minded man (person) is unstable in all of his (or her) ways." (NASB)

b. Living in a constant state of compromise causes us to be emotionally stuck and leaves us wondering why we are not able to progress in life. Double-mindedness creates blockages in our ability to accomplish goals and dreams, and disables us from truly pursuing and reaching purpose. Rather than swaying back and forth, begin developing a love and trust for God's Word. Develop a concrete decision regarding your standards. Once that decision is made, you won't have to consider the compromise when questionable opportunities are presented.

7. *Disobedience*

a. The device of disobedience is best described as the purposeful decision to refuse to follow directives or the instructions of authority. Disobedience is a matter of pride. Whether we disobey the "Stop" sign at the corner, the instruction of our manager at work, or the teaching of the Word of God in the Bible, it all related to the fact that we think we know better or have an easier or more logical solution than the one presented. We are deceived and expose ourselves to endless danger when we ignore direction given by those in authority. Proverbs 16:18 reminds us that "pride goes before destruction, and a haughty spirit before stumbling." (NASB)

b. In disobedience, we strive to prove our own way, our self-worth, and our boastful knowledge of life without adequately considering how mistaken we are. This device causes us to be estranged from those who care for us, leaving us alone to bear the consequences of poor choices. Disobedience to God causes blindness to God's purpose and provision for our lives. This prideful response cripples our ability to learn from the experiences of others rather than being humble and available to be coached and mentored by those who have more experience and insight than we do.

Part 3
OPEN BOOK TEST

When you consider the choice to WALK or BEND, you must know that God wants the absolute best for you. Deuteronomy 30:19 encourages, "Today I have given you the choice between life and death, between blessings and curses. Now I call on heaven and earth to witness the choice you make. Oh, that you would choose life, so that you and your descendants might live!" (NLT)

This sincere plea made on behalf of God clearly outlines the available choices. Then He tells which choice He hopes you will make and then makes you a promise of longevity if you will follow. With all of that said, He still loves you enough to allow you to make the decision. We do not have to be ensnarled by these devices, nor do we have to continue to be entangled by the grips of unresolved rejection. We just have to make the decision to WALK and realize that we are accepted into the beloved family of God.

I must admit, it took me some time to fully realize and accept that God completely and unconditionally accepted me. At first, I didn't really understand what that acceptance really meant. All of the examples of acceptance that I had experienced in life were so superficial and temporary. I wondered,

> We do not have to be ensnarled by these devices, nor do we have to continue to be entangled by the grips of unresolved rejection.

Was it like when someone gives you a gift that you don't really prefer, but you take it as a show of kindness then shove it in the back of the closet? Was this the type of acceptance that was good for the moment, but as soon as something better came along, I was tossed aside to make room for the upgrade? Was it the acceptance that comes with endless words of loyalty and availability, but when a real need arose the person was nowhere to be found, abandoning all of their promises?

These were the kinds of acceptance I experienced. I can't tell you how many times, I have felt shoved into a closet, tossed aside for an upgrade, and abandoned—all by people and situations that assured me that I was accepted. I wasn't sure how it could be possible for God, in all of His glory and holiness, to want to accept me. In fact, I really didn't think I mattered that much God at all. I thought I had to prove my value and worth to God in order for Him to love me. I was constantly trying to fix myself, trying to become the "perfect" Christian to earn His love.

I recently moved. Through the process of packing and unpacking my office, I began reviewing the books that I have collected over the years. My books have the date I received them written in the first few pages. Each of the book titles and the dates chronicled my process of trying to learn how to be "good enough" for God to love me. There are books on prayer, fasting, obedience, and all sorts of other ministry tools in my catalog of books. There is nothing wrong with understanding these topics, but in my case and at that time, I was learning from them for the wrong reasons.

The devices of disappointment, discouragement, and deceit were in full effect in my life. Not only had they affected my relationship with others, they were now crippling my relationship with

God. I was BENDing and could not understand why
life—and accepting my acceptance—was so hard.

Part 4

WALK INTO FREEDOM

P icture yourself in a box. In the beginning, the box is very large and you have space to move around the box as freely as you choose. Over time, the box seems to get smaller and smaller. Your space is becoming limited. The longer you stay in the box, the more cramped you become.

Each day you develop a pattern of moving around in the confined space. Since the box is too short for you to fully stand up, you move with your head lowered to make sure you don't brush your head on the ceiling. The box is not wide enough for you to extend your arms out on each side, so you make small, concentrated movements that fall within the width of your body. Your arms, legs, and back still have full range of motion, but since there is no space and bigger movements are met with pain, why bother?

One day, the walls of the box are taken away. Your head is down, focusing on your concentrated, small movements, and you never notice that there is more light and there are other people moving around you. You are still leaning forward as if the box were still there. Someone comes and asks you why you always have your head down and make such small movements. Your only reply is that it hurts too much to do it any other way.

That is exactly where I was—living a confined life in a mental and emotional box. Rejection created the box and I inhabited that space, allowing it to squeeze and limit every part of my being. The truth is, Jesus came to set me free and removed the walls of the box, but I had not realized my freedom. I was a Christian and still confined by unresolved rejection. I was a Christian and still seeking external Triple A. I was a Christian and still filling voids to avoid feeling the void that only the acceptance of God's unconditional love could completely occupy.

That day when the truth of God's Word in Ephesians 1:6 ("To the praise of the glory of his grace, wherein he hath made us accepted in the beloved") (KJV) leapt off the page and pierced my heart, I finally knew the truth. I could finally, fully stand in the fact that God loves me and that Jesus died for me to give me the gift of salvation. There was nothing I needed to do, or could do, to deserve or earn God's love and acceptance of me. It was a gift freely given to me.

Now I could Willfully Abandon the Lies and Know (WALK) the truth. I willfully committed to accepting God's undying love for me and believing everything that God says about me. I have abandoned the lies told to me and those that I constructed on my own. Most importantly, I know the truth of God's Word concerning His plan and purpose for my life.

Section 3– Points to Ponder

1. I want to encourage you to know that you, too, can stop BENDing and begin WALKing the truth.

2. Consider the devices that you have experienced in life (before and after salvation). Which of these devices are still

at work in your life?

3. List the way you can begin to dismantle your belief in and active participation in these devices.

4. Commit to making the choice to WALK instead of BEND.

Section 3– Let's Pray

Heavenly Father, thank you for loving me and accepting me. I ask that you help me fully accept your acceptance. Thank you for setting me free from all of the things that have confined me. I realize that I have allowed myself to remain entrapped by the rejections that I have experienced. Please forgive me for the mistakes that I have made and for hurting others as I was trying to find my way. Father, I ask that you guide me as I WALK into your freedom. Continue to allow my heart to be healed by your Word and allow our relationship to grow closer, through your love. I am grateful that as I continue to WALK closer with you, every broken place in me and in my life is being restored and made whole. Thank you, Father and I love you.

In Jesus's Name. Amen.

Section 4

WALKing in Wisdom

Holland B. Nance

Part 1

HOW LONG WILL YOU MOURN?

Be very careful, then, how you live—not as unwise but as wise, making the most of every opportunity, because the days are evil. Ephesians 5:15-16 (NIV)

I n I Samuel 16, we read a gripping discussion between God and the prophet Samuel that begins with the question, "How long will you mourn over Saul?" You see, Samuel was disheartened that Saul (the first king of Israel) disobeyed and displeased God during his final years. Since Saul rejected God's Word, God rejected Saul as king. Samuel was so disappointed and filled with grief, prompting God to come to Samuel and pose this serious question.

The same should be asked of us: "How long will we mourn?" Yes, we have experienced heartbreak, betrayal, and disappointment. No, we were not always loved and protected by those who should have done a better job at caring for us. Yes, we were rejected, dejected, left out, picked on, criticized, misjudged, taken for granted, and then pushed aside. All of those things happened. Nevertheless, how long will we sit in the seat of despair and anguish over the events of our past? How long will we allow these truths of our past to dictate the potential of our future? How long will we take the position of the victim, oppressed by the memories of what was and what could have been? It is time that we put an end to this series of events.

God asked Samuel a tough question, but in this conversation, we find so much hope to help us transition from our position of mourning. First Samuel 16:1 says, "Now the LORD said to Samuel, 'How long will you grieve over Saul, since I have rejected him from being king over Israel? Fill your horn with oil and go; I will send you to Jesse the Bethlehemite, for I have selected a king for Myself among his sons.'" (NASB) Here, God gives three powerful pieces of information and instruction.

The first is to know God's perspective on the situation. It was clear that God said He rejected Saul as king, but Samuel was still mourning. They key to focus on here is whether our opinion on the matter matches God's viewpoint. The job promotion may have passed you over, but was that the opportunity God had planned for you, or was there another, even better promotion coming along later? The relationship did not progress in the way you hoped, but was that relationship the one that would honor God and all that He has designed for your life? It is so important that we begin to see the idiosyncrasies of our life from God's perspective. He knows the end from the very beginning. Just because something looks, feels, and seems good right now, it may lead to the dismantling of what God is building for your future.

The second important note is that God gave Samuel a specific instruction to "fill your horn with oil and go." This was intended to assure Samuel that just because the circumstances with Saul didn't work out the way he hoped, God hadn't fired Samuel from his role as the prophet and hadn't stripped him of the responsibility of anointing the king. God told him to gather the supplies necessary to go and continue living out his purpose. For us, we need to have a close connection with the Word of God through Bible study

[?]

and close communication with God through prayers. We can equip and educate ourselves in every way imaginable, but if we do not fill ourselves with these life-building and equipping elements, we will lack the essential pieces that will carry us to our purpose. As we continually prepare ourselves with knowledge of the Word of God and prayer, we can see more clearly and move forward toward our purpose.

The third critical point here is that God lays out specific instructions that will lead to the fulfillment of His true purpose. Once Samuel goes, God's predetermined strategy unfolded right before him. Samuel simply needed to go and follow instructions. We all should know that God has a new plan to reveal to us. When we share our hurts and pains with Him, He responds with love and yet compels us to move forward. The amazing thing is that He provides

> All we have to know is that once we start moving in alignment with our purpose, God's plan will begin to unfold.

us insight on His new plan. There is no need for us to strategize on the next tactics to achieve the goal we have been pursuing for years. We don't have to manipulate any situation to shift the outcome in our favor. All we have to know is that once we start moving in alignment with our purpose, God's plan will begin to unfold.

Samuel has an open and honest conversation with God about what was causing him such emotional pain. God heard his heart and provided Samuel with the assurance that he was still entrusted to carry out his purpose for his life. Even after God laid out His precise plan, Samuel still expressed concern and fear. We should know that God is aware of every worry, anxiety, and frustration we face. He has an empathetic ear regarding those issues and is willing to help us make the transition from the position of mourning and pain to a place of productive progression toward our purpose.

Life can be difficult and oftentimes presents us with experiences that leave us feeling just like Samuel. The disappointments and feelings of rejection can be overwhelming, so much so that we live in confinement and are trapped in the framework of self-defeating coping tendencies. While the events of the past are real, we must come to a point where we place an expiration date on those effects. Once we take a moment and address the issues that have caused pain and heartbreak, we must be committed to truly allowing ourselves the advantage of emotional and spiritual development. To fully progress along the journey of WALKing toward freedom, we must end the mourning period and prepare ourselves to move forward.

Part 2

MOVING FROM VOID
TO VICTORY

The journey of WALKing from rejection to freedom is also an ongoing process. Yes, you will be confronted with rejection again. The difference is now, you have the tools to help you respond in an empowering way. No longer will you be debilitated by rejection. You will acknowledge that pain, pick out the pieces that cause you to grown, and prepare for what comes next. You will be strengthened to make the necessary modifications and allow God to refine you, your skills and your goals so that when the next opportunity is presented, you are ready to win! First Corinthians 15:57 reminds you, "but thanks be God!

He gives us [you] the victory through our Lord Jesus Christ." (NASB)

The test of victory for me is the fact that I am still "Helpful Holland". I love being available to assist others. I still volunteer at my church and with community organizations. I still participate in committee meetings and share insights on strategic planning. I still enjoy giving gifts to my friends and loved ones. The difference now is the motivation. No longer is it done with the purpose of winning favor or to be liked. I no longer look for these opportunities as ways to meet my Triple A needs. My Lord and Savior, Jesus Christ met my need for acceptance, approval, and affirmation when He chose to allow Himself to be wounded for my transgressions and bruised for my iniquities (*paraphrased* Isaiah 53:3). That level of love is unmatched and incomparable to any "thank you" note or pat on the back I can ever receive. This has allowed me to discover the true joy in authentically being the person God has created me to be.

Love has occupied that God-sized void that was meant only for Him to fill. First John 4:8 states emphatically, "God is love." (NASB) This love must penetrate the core of your heart and soul. Allow God's love to fill every empty and dark space where the residue of rejection tries to reside. Begin to realize how valuable you are to God—that He would sacrifice His only Son in such a gruesome way just so He could have a close, personal relationship with you.

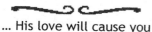

... His love will cause you to leap out of boxes of emotional and spiritual confinement and began pursuing your purpose.

Understand how much you matter to God and that He is aware of every part of who you are. It is amazing the efforts many will take to win the love of another person who barely acknowledges their existence while the calls of the Creator of the Universe continue to go ignored.

As our relationship with God grows, He continues to pour out His love on us. This is done not just in the big ways, like allowing us to live each new day and providing for our daily needs, but also in the special intimate ways like when He prepares an unexpected gift or "surprise" during the day that answers a quietly whispered prayer or request from the heart. That is when we begin to truly feel the magnitude of the acceptance and love our Heavenly Father has for us.

Victory comes with knowing that acceptance comes from God and not any external source. No matter what anyone says or does, or whether you are promoted or not, and even when you are ignored, you can always pull from God's internal wellspring of acceptance, joy, love, and peace as your source of empowerment. The confidence you will begin to feel will be astounding! This will allow you to be willing to try more and to engage in new and old relationships from a more authentic and less dependent perspective. The freedom in knowing that you are following the leading of the Spirit of God with the reinforcement of His love will cause you to leap out of boxes of emotional and spiritual confinement and begin pursuing your purpose.

Part 3

TRAIN YOURSELF
TO WALK

This journey of WALKing is not an automatic response. It is easy to slide into habitual behaviors that represent the confined lifestyle. We can certainly be confronted with rejection and begin to internalize feelings of insufficiency and unworthiness. Rejection still hurts, the difference is you now are equipped to know that there is no need to sign a lease for a new box within which to confine yourself.

You must TRAIN yourself on how to WALK in freedom. The best way to do this is to re-map how you think in these situations. Romans 12:2 encourages you to be "transformed by the renewing of your mind." (NASB) Just like when someone is trying to improve their physical fitness they must train their bodies to endure uncommon activities to build strength and endurance; we must do the same when it comes to WALKing from rejection to freedom.

TRAINing is not a one and done procedure. It takes intentionality and persistence. Here's how to do it:

1. **T—Talk** with God about everything that concerns you (Pray). One of my favorite scriptures is Psalm 138:8. It says, "The Lord will accomplish what concerns me." This open communication builds intimacy and trust with the lover of your soul. Many believe that there are matters too trivial to discuss with God, but I strongly disagree. The God who made us cares about every molecule of our being. In fact, Luke 12:7 assures us, "Indeed, the very hairs of your head are all numbered. Do not fear; you are more valuable than many sparrows." (NIV) Just know that God loves you and invites you to "cast all your anxiety

on Him, because He cares for you." (I Peter 5:7) (NIV)

2. **R—Read** the Word of God to understand God's perspective on your concerns. This is critical for providing your mind and thought process with the right tools to begin to modify your thinking. It is easy to naturally come up with solutions to problems, but still get the same results. Yet you will experience breakthrough when you seek God's vantage point and apply the principles relayed through His Word. Jesus even used this method when He was being tempted by the devil. He responded with, "Man shall not live on bread alone, but on every word that proceeds out of the mouth of God." (Matthew 4:4) (NASB)

3. **A—Allow** the power of the Holy Spirit to speak to your heart and give you insights on what God wants you to do (or does not want you to do) about the concern. We are invited constantly to inquire of the Holy Spirit to gain knowledge and discernment. First Corinthians 2:9-10 states, "What no eye has seen, what no ear has heard, and what no human mind has

conceived the things God has prepared for those who love Him these are the things God has revealed to us by his Spirit. The Spirit searches all things, even the deep things of God." (NIV)

4. I—**Invite** people who think and speak positively into your life. God has made us relational beings and we need to be connected to others. The trouble arises when the others we choose to spend time with continue to feed our debilitating attributes. It is so difficult to change your way of thinking, and constantly talking with and spending time with people who are not thinking or behaving in ways that do not support your new mindset is harmful. First Corinthians 15:33 reminds us, "Do not be misled: Bad company corrupts good character." (NIV) To begin WALKing in a new direction, we have to engage in the company of those who support our move toward freedom. Pray and seek friendships, mentors, and coaches who will encourage you

and remind you of the benefits of this transformative life.

5. **N—Nurture** an emotional atmosphere for elevated thinking. Years ago when I was learning to write computer code languages, the professor often used the phrase "garbage in, garbage out". This meant that if I entered bad code, I'd get bad results or an error in my output. The same is true when we are renewing our minds. Proverbs 4:23 instructs us, "Watch over your heart with all diligence, For from it flow the springs of life." (NASB) We must be mindful of what we expose ourselves to; every television program, song, commercial, advertisement, and online post can have subliminal messaging that can seep into the crevices of our hearts and sow seeds of discord, insecurity, lust, envy, and a number of other feelings that do not propel our lives in the direction of freedom.

WALKing in Wisdom requires the focus to take a realistic approach regarding our history with rejection. Taking into consideration that once the past instances are addressed and healed so that the confinement of rejection is eradicated, these things have no power or influence to limit our potential. Instead, these experiences should be the launching point to drive our progression forward with even more vigor. Freedom is restored and recovered for the sole objective of living in our purpose—and our commitments to sustaining this freedom has to be the stimulus of developing daily disciplines that will facilitate our journey of WALKing.

Section4– Points to Ponder

1. What experiences are you committed to mourn about no longer?
2. Consider the revelation of God's new plan for your life. What instructions has He given you?
3. How can you see the victory taking form in your life?
4. Commit to begin TRAINing consistently.

Section 4 – Let's Pray

Heavenly Father, thank you for caring about everything that concerns me. I trust you and know that you are working all of these thing together for my good. Father, I ask you to reveal to me the next steps to take as I walk out your plan for my life. Help me to know clearly what decisions to make. I ask that you send positive friendships, mentors, and coaches into my life so that I can continue living in the victory you have given. I need your help in being a good steward over all of the gifts, talents, abilities, and the freedom you have provided. Thank you for healing my heart, more and more each day.

In Jesus's Name. Amen.

Section 5

An Open Letter to Fathers

When I began writing this book, years ago, I recalled watching news stories about young female celebrities who were not wearing appropriate attire and exposing too much of themselves to gain additional attention. I thought, *why do something like that, with all the advantages they have in life? They must have daddy issues. I have others issues, sure, but at least I don't have daddy issues.*

As the writing continued and God began to reveal more of *my* issues, I realized how wrong I was. I did have daddy issues. For those with unresolved matters with fathers, those who have loving relationships with fathers, or for fathers who need to hear from their children, may this open letter provide a perspective on the many things that often go unsaid.

AN OPEN LETTER TO FATHERS

D ear Father (Dad, Stepdad, Male Role Model),

Let me begin by saying two of the most important words in this entire letter; thank you. Thank you for being my father, for without you, I would not exist or be the person I am now. I want you to know how important your role as a father is to me. It may seem that you are often ignored or made to feel like an afterthought, but you really are one of the most important people in my life. I appreciate you for being a part of my life in the ways that you were.

No, you were not perfect and neither was I. Sometimes I judged you too harshly and I frequently expected you to be my strong superhero without giving you an opportunity to display any weakness or frailty. At times, I was disappointed and angry; other times I was elated just to hear your voice. There were times when you wanted to spend time and talk with me and I was not available or was too busy. Then there were those times when you wanted to protect me and you held back what you wished you could say. Just know that I was stronger than you thought and always hoped that one day you would really share what was on your heart.

You gave me so much. Through you, I learned resilience, tenacity, patience, faith, and the ability to keep trying until I mastered what I wanted to accomplish. You showed me a picture of what life could be with or without you. You informed my creativity and caused my personality to blossom. From you I learned the importance of truth and integrity. I learned how to be strong when everything in me wanted to curl up and cry. You showed me what it meant to have a strong work ethic and the importance of being a provider for the family.

Some of these things you actually did and some you did not. There were days when you were present, right by my side to provide comfort and protection, and other days your absence filled every fiber of my being. There are times when I can hear your familiar voice reminding me of the lessons you taught, even when you were miles away. Other times, I simply wish I knew how your voice sounded.

I am grateful for all of it—the good, the bad, and the indifferent. Every part of how your life influences me is a part of God's plan for both of us. You, being the father you are, created the hunger for our Heavenly Father. I really did need a father like you to love a Father like Him. A Father like Him showed me how to love a father like you.

Regardless of the details, always know that you are loved.

-Your child.

RESOURCES

Want to know Jesus?
1-888-NEED-HIM

Grace Help Line
1-800-982-8032

National Association
of Adult Survivors of Child Abuse
www.naasca.org/

RAINN (Rape, Abuse & Incest National Network)
www.rainn.org
1-800-656-HOPE (4673)

National Christian Counselors Association
1-941-388-6868

Association of Christian Counselors
1-800-526-8673

Crisis Pregnancy Hotline
1-800-67-BABY-6

Post Abortion Counseling
1-800-228-0332

Stop it Now!
1-888-PREVENT

RESOURCES

S.A.F.E. (Self-Abuse Finally Ends)
1-800-DONT-CUT

Suicide Hotline
1-800-273-TALK (8255)

Suicide Prevention Hotline
1-800-827-7571

National Domestic Violence Hotline
1-800-799-SAFE

Battered Women and their Children
1-800=603-HELP

Eating Disorders Awareness and Prevention
1-800-931-2237

Compulsive Gambling Hotline
1-410-332-0402

Focus on the Family (Sexual Addictions)
1-800-A-FAMILY

GriefShare
1-800-395-5755

Grace Help Line
1-800-982-8032

CPSIA information can be obtained
at www.ICGtesting.com
Printed in the USA
LVOW13s1457280217
525583LV00017B/18/P